A Day in the Life of a C

Anne Goodfriend

Contents

Rigby®

A Harcourt Achieve Imprint

www.Rigby.com

1-800-531-5015

Making Life Easier

Computers make life easier because people can use them to do many things.

You can use a computer to write a letter or send a message.

You can use a computer to make pictures, play games, and do many more things!

This family has a computer at home.

Everyone in the family can use the computer.

Let's see how this family uses the computer in one day.

family with a computer

 Working at Home

It's 7:00 in the morning.
Mom works at home as a
writer for a local newspaper.
She checks her **e-mail** and finds
a message from the newspaper
because they want her to write
an article about dogs.
Mom knows a lot about dogs.
She writes back,
"Yes, I'll write the article."

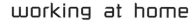
working at home

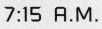 Paying Bills

Mom can also use the computer to pay bills.

Today she'll pay the phone bill and the electric bill.

It's easy to pay bills using the computer.

paying bills

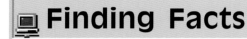

Finding Facts

Later that morning, Lina uses the
Internet to find facts about
sea turtles on the computer.
Lina finds a good **Web site**
with great pictures of sea turtles.
She prints out the pages that
are most helpful.
Finding facts with a computer
is fast and easy.
Lina will write the report when
she gets to school.

finding facts

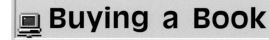

Buying a Book

Now Grandma uses the computer.
Grandma would like to buy a book about
sea animals for Lina.
She finds a book on the Internet
and orders it.
It would have taken Grandma a lot
more time to go to a bookstore and
look for a book.
It's easy to buy a book using
a computer, isn't it?

buying a book

Books.Com

Our Price $6.95
In Stock

Sea Animals

To buy this book,
click below

Add to Cart

2:00 P.M.

🖳 Taking Classes

It's 2:00 P.M., and now Manuel uses
the computer.
He is taking a class from home.
He can read whole lessons
on the computer from home.
He can also e-mail his teacher and send
his homework using the computer.

taking classes

Class Schedules

Green Hills
Community
College

Biology 101
• Week three

Search   Info   Contact   What's New!

Doing Math

Dad builds houses.

He uses the computer when he gets home.

First he lists the items he needs to build a house.

Dad also inputs the cost of each item.

Then he uses the computer to add all the numbers.

It's easy to do math with a computer.

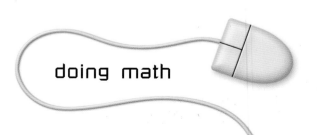

doing math

8:00 P.M.

 Keeping in Touch

After dinner Mom checks her e-mail again.
She finds a message from her sister Marta.
Marta lives in a different city and
has sent the family a message with a picture.
Mom prints the picture and calls the rest
of the family to share it.
It's easy to keep in touch with family and
friends when you use a computer.
This family uses the computer to do
many things for school, work, or fun.
Computers really do make life easier!

keeping
in touch

 Glossary

computers   machines that store, use, and show information

e-mail   messages people send using computers

Internet   a way to let people around the world use computers to share information

Web site   a page on the Internet that has information